NAKED CITY BLUES

Chan. McKenzie

Copyright © 2008 Chandra McKenzie

No part of this book may be copied, reproduced, or used in any way without written permission from the author.

This book was printed by:

ColorCentric Corporation
100 Carlson Road
Rochester, NY 14610

McKenzie, Chan. (Chandra)
   Naked city blues / Chan. McKenzie. –
     p. cm. --
     ISBN 978-0-6152-0330-0

PS3563.A31588N35 2008

Printed in the United States of America

Lulu URL: http://stores.lulu.com/ChanMcKenzieStorefront

Also by Chan. McKenzie

Implications

In A Quandary

This is for pops, Harlie who whispered words in my ear.
This is for moms, Ruby who kept her hand at my back.
This is for Gram, Edna who gave me reasons to smile.
This is for Dorthea, who cares for my everything else.

CONTENTS

Bluesis	11
Greatest Hits	13
At The Blue Note	15
Bars	17
Doing Okay	19
I Stood Up	21
Piper's Blues	23
Promises of Daydreams	25
Black Girls Like Me	27
Lineage	29
Notes to My Son	31
Coz	33
Sunny Side of the Street	35
Tired Feet	37
A Lovers Indignation	39
Last Word	41
NYC	43
Robb, the Last Time	45
Notes To A Man Friend	47
Sensitive Woman	49
Complications	51
Legal Tender	53
Turn Up the Music	55
Fiesta	57
Rush	59
Preludes	61
Sparrow Contemplates the Seasons	63
Midnight Hour	65
Art of Leaving In the Morning	67
She Is Here	69
Conflict	71
Loving Your Behind	73
An Unforeseen Circumstance	75
The Last of You	77
Grown Up Conclusions	79
Troubles	81
Life's Work	83
Pen Is Stuck	85
Testify	87
Simple	89

NAKED CITY BLUES

BLUESIS

A blues is
when somebody bangs hard
on your heart
and then disappears.

A blues is
when there is a lot of
open space around you,
but you still feel confined.

A blues cuts deeply,
heals slowly,
and
bleeds intermittently.

A blues is
when you don't know;
You don't want to know;
and not knowing
is just fine -
Period.

A blues is
not necessarily definable.
It's just a feeling.
It feels like a hum.

Rocking back and forth
works best,
when you got one.

GREATEST HITS

With the flip of a switch
they take a horse
and shove it insistently
into Billie's brown arm.

Then in a slow, throaty murmur
she raises her semi-conscious head
and the song
without force,
begins to sing itself.

This lady, Blues
sits on my lap
with her heavy arms
draped round my shoulder.

She weighs me down
like an obese lover
perspiring.
Her pain is all around me.

I blow lofty smoke rings
full of near perfect sadness
across the creases
in her forehead.

We hum together,
Gloomy Sunday...

AT THE BLUE NOTE

The scar born of a razor's edge
pokes prominently
across his pudgy cheek.

"This happened one night," he reminisces
almost fondly.
Then he proceeds to bear witness to
the fury of a good woman scorned
by a young man's inconsideration.

1946,
in a bar called the Blue Note.

He still remembers the moment
Lil burst through the door.
He cannot recall
the name of that *"sweet young gal"*
he was dancing with
at the time.

Suddenly,
couples scattered around them.
Chairs were pushed back for better viewing.
A knowing hush fell across the room.
Everyone else had seen Lil enter.

Although it seemed a long way
from the door to dance floor,
actually he had only one minute
to push his date away.
His righteous indignation
met Lil's anger eye to eye.

In retrospect he knows
the woman he faced that night,
had not come in search of explanations.

*"I haven't seen
nor heard from Lil in forty years,"* he says
rubbing an old man hand
up and down the side of his winkled face.
*"She sure got all she wanted from me that night.
Yes sir, I learned that lesson well."*

A good-hearted woman
with the best intentions,
won't take kindly to a foolish man
who won't keep her love
foremost on his mind.

"BARS

Hi.

Hi...oh, hi! Jesus. Man, it's been a long time. How're you doing?

Good. Good. How about you?

I'm good. So, uh- what's been happening?

Oh nothing much, really. What's news with you?

Well, you know- same old thing, Man. You know how it is.

Yeah. Definitely. I surely do.

    [Uncomfortable pause]

It's really crowded in here tonight, isn't it?

Yes, it is.

Must be a full moon or something.

    [Ha-Ha]

Yeah, you got that right.

Right.

Say, have you seen [fill in the blank] *in here tonight?*

Yes - uh , oh, over there by the bar.

Oh yeah – Good. Thanks. Well, listen I'll catch up with you later then, okay?

Sure thing you take care.

Listen, don't be such a stranger.

It was really great to see you.

Yes. Right. Same here.

DOING OKAY

Doing okay
I managed to say.
When she asked
how I was doing,
without including
how was I doing-

NOW THAT YOU...

EVER SINCE YOU...

WITHOUT YOU...

I wanted to be prepared
because I knew
someone would ask me.
Someone we knew-
someone who knew.

But I was not ready
when she asked me.
So it caught me off guard.
All I could manage
was to clear my throat
and force the words to form.

"Okay!" I told her much too quickly.

"Doing okay!" I replied.

"I'm doing just fine!" I said again,
In case she missed it, but
I know that
she knows that
I lied.

I STOOD UP

I stood up
in front of all these strangers
knowing good and well
that I was drunk
and had no business
forcing my sorrow on unsuspecting people.
But I was hurtin'
and got carried away by the moment.

So I stood up,
in the middle of a crowded bar,
at six-thirty on a Friday evening,
on the fourteenth day of November,
and I wailed out a few lines of
Empty Bed Blues,
just as loud as you please.

I swear you might have thought
I was Bessie, born again.
I had a blues Chile,
and couldn't nothing
keep me from singing out loud
for the world to know about it.

Sure it sounds strange
but I'm not crazy.

There's just something about a broken heart
that can make you do the unexpected.

PIPER'S BLUES

Son,
you need to be wise
'bout how high a price
you risk for your
creative inspiration.
The mean old dirty blues
cost pieces of your core.

At two am you're bleeding,
just when you thought
there was no more.
The muse
for the best thing
you play and loose,
will never be satiated
by one night's composition.

You go 'head and play my man,
and remember what I say,
what looks good on the upside
may pull you down some day.

Your time will come on key.
the piper's blues once summoned
won't never leave you be.

I say
old piper's blues
once rendered,
won't never set you free.

PROMISES OF DAYDREAMS

Underneath the places
where this clown strikes appealing poses
for public consumption,
a little girl lives who fears strangers.
Behind the bravado
and the tempered gusto
there is one so small
as to lack significance.
This young gal,
this tender youth,
extends trusting fragile feelings
to bridge the dark places filled with
unfamiliar faces.
No,
I am not Joan of Arc and
I shall never be such a woman
as Mary Macleod Bethune.
All I have is
a sensitive separate portion,
and it makes me vulnerable to you.
Underneath my little places,
where this desire for recognition resides,
a small girl dwells,
quietly relying on
the promises of daydreams.

BLACK GIRLS LIKE ME

three blonde girls
kids together
friends for life,
they can succeed
they will achieve
most choices
theirs for selection...

>*what is the plan for
black girls like me?*

three blonde girls
debs together
friends for life
they'll be radiant,
slender and fine,
cool beauties
turn heads and walk by...

>*why are eyes closed for
black girls like me?*

three blonde girls
coeds together
friends for life
the top ten schools
summer in Europe
dates to spare
dad gives her away...

>*where are the doors for
black girls like me?*

three blonde girls
wives' together
friends for life.
babies grow up
days come and go
wrinkles show
life's ordered fashion...

>*who'll make a way for
black girls like me?*

*Who will pave the way for
black girls like me?*

Black girls, like me.

LINEAGE

We were all given away
in one way or another.
What a strange discovery
this knowledge that I come from
a line of not orphans
whose mothers had to let them go
temporarily,
for reasons beyond their control.

My grandmother.
My father.
Myself.
Set early wondering where Mama had gone,
leaving us behind in this place called,
"the best I can do for right now."
Not truly comprehending in children's terms
what *'temporary"* held in store.

My grandmother was the oldest one.
She did not look like her brothers and sisters.
She was too light to fit in right
in her mother's husband's home.
She still remembers
getting off the boat in her Sunday best,
where distant relations had come to meet her.
No one was there who explained,
what *"temporary"* would really mean,
but she could feel it in her heart.
She had to work for her daily keep,
and she was never to feel welcomed.
That was 1921
and home was soon a long way gone
in a young girl's eyes.

THIS LINK
BECOMES
MY OWN
CONNECTION

1934, a young woman bundles two small children
at the train station,
my father and his sister.
There is no money to give them,
two weeks work already owed
has purchased their one way tickets
to her dead husband's family down south.
She did not expect her children to understand
but inside she knew.
She put them on a train
with a kiss and a hug goodbye,
and did not try to explain
rents overdue,

daddy's debts to pay off
scrubbing somebody's floors
even if it would mean
kneeling all day on her bad knee.
They wept and clung to her,
but she did not let them see her cry.
Nor did she say,
"This is just temporary."
Recollection told her,
it was the best she could do for right now.

THIS LINK
BECOMES
MY OWN
CONNECTION.

I was just a baby
when I rode that long day and a half trip,
perched safely on my grandma's lap.
It was just fine with me
because my grandma spoiled me rotten.
If I understand correctly
my mother was ill
and couldn't care for me just then.

What I remember is,
I lived with Gram for five years
and I didn't know enough
to really miss my mama.

THIS LINK
BECOMES
MY OWN
CONNECTION

The differences were never reconciled.
Mothers sacrificed children for the sake of
getting by.
We were all reclaimed in time,
but the gaps did not fill themselves easily.

I do not pretend to know
the full effect
time left behind
had on each of us in turn.

What I know is,
I come from a lineage
of little faces
waving goodbye
to a moving figure
standing on the platform.

NOTES TO MY SON

I haven't lost weight yet,
and no one keeled over and left me a million dollars.
So, I cannot tell you that the best of everything
is going to be yours just for the asking.

I'm not perfect.
Though you undoubtedly will be,
the moment we first lay eyes on you in the hospital.
That will keep us afloat, at least until the
fiftieth time there is nothing in the potty.

I have no guarantee that I'll become the kind of super mother
you'll remember with a tear
once I am dead and gone.
All I have to give to you is the very best of my intentions,
Though some days, even they may have to take a back seat
to other things which will demand my divided attention.

You'll have to work when you get old enough, just like I do
and you'll have to save money to have money, just like I did,
and get used to it because
we're going to be driving around in an old car, at least for now.
I haven't found a fool proof way to ensure all my good answers
don't get used up well before you're fifteen and know it all.
You're going to have to hear 'because I said so' at least a few hundred times.
And though you won't like it, I plan on saying 'No' whenever I need to
and it's okay with me if you quietly disagree.
Sometimes, I won't understand why either,
but I'll be feeling my way through so
no will be the way we go and
no will stand, despite your pouts and protestations.

You're going to bed early,
and I'm not handing out an allowance every week.
You have to make your bed and
help with chores
even when you don't feel like it.
You'll have to introduce me to your friends,
especially the cool ones you know I won't like.

Oh and I'll expect you to be responsible
and by the way,
you're going to college,
so pick one.

There is going to be a solar eclipse this Christmas,
and the man who will be your first president
believes you're better off
without your Mami-to be and me as parents.
Someday we'll discuss all this.
I just pray by then I'll have found the right words
to help you understand how much we want you.

Meanwhile,
all we can guarantee you is lots of hugs,
a place where you will always belong,
and a loving family bond which you will never have to question.

Everything other than that,
we'll have to figure out together,
tomorrow,
after you're born.

COZ

You gave birth
and then
lost your love
the hard way.

I wrote poems
and am just beginning
to be responsible for them.

You are
younger.

I have gotten old.

We are a year apart
but now a long way separated.

Momee,
these words of mine
are not as beautiful
as your little boy.

My love for you
still remains deep
like a river my friend.

Surely Chile,
humph,

YOU KNOW IT!

We will always be,

One
baaaad

And

Two
cooool.

SUNNY SIDE OF THE STREET

When I was younger-
perhaps seven, maybe eight,
I was surrounded by cousins.
I was the youngest
by consequence of birth.
There was nothing else for me to do
but constantly try to prove myself worthy
of their inner circle.

At thirteen
all the cool kids in the neighborhood
thought Mapes Avenue was the place to be.
So did I,
but none of the cool kids
wanted to go there
with me.

I was sixteen
when I realized
my father could not be resurrected.
I would have to face myself
and all my furies
to deal with the fates
I was handed.

I am not saying
I had hard knocks
cause I know plenty others
who have had it harder than me.
I had my brains, my books and
enough unfulfilled desire
to want to stay free
until the highway could lead me away
from my mother's constant influence.

Suddenly,
it became clearer
that it was up to me
not to kill myself
trying to be bad all at once.

I believe somebody was watching out for me.
I will always swear it was Pops.
Lord knows I could have been dead so many times
cause I was always one to reach for the fire.

Today I find myself
surrendering to everyday realization.
I know now that I was not meant
to burn big holes in the scheme of things.

I will always be that little girl from Tremont Avenue
running crazy in the summer heat.
I don't know much about grass being greener
but I do know enough, finally,
not to dart out into the street.

TIRED FEET

Mom and I are the same person,
and it bothers both of us sometimes.

I never thought I would admit this
because there was a time when I swore
I would never be like her when I grew up.

Now I find
that I get moody too,
just for the hell of it.
Sometimes I get damn tired
of having to be responsible.
So I understand
that some of those times,
when she didn't have time,
are like the time
that I don't have now.

I used to be a wild child
feverish with the desire to digress
from each mainstream notion
she offered up for me.

These days
I get home from work
and I can't even stand the possibility that
the phone may ring.

I remember Momma
and it makes me wonder why I,
the oldest of three she raised alone,
ever once begrudged having to lug
a bucket filled with warm faucet water
to what surely must have been
some very tired feet.

A LOVER'S INDIGNATION

You keep making me
look at my own Black self
wondering why
you can get so angry
while I can act like I didn't see them.

You keep telling me
these opposing forces
are all around us and
you want me to be more aware.

I want you to realize
that they have already made emotional contact.
...and yes babe it does bother me
when people try call me NIGGER.
NIGGA disregards my humanity.
They want me to inhabit an identity
they say is mine to belong in.
But I have been taught never to flinch,
own,
or be owned by that word.

This is my defense
against an ignorant evil,
passed down to me
with insistence
by prior generations
who walked more treacherous miles
than mine.

So yes honey, I walk on
Nothing said, nothing registered with me.
My pride is stubborn
My anger righteous
My reaction controlled.
Defiance is in my eyes.

You want to try and steel me
against words meant to
break my spirit.
But no one could protect Martin
so, I know I
am not safe or steadied
hiding behind your loving indignation.

My fortress is already inside me,
genealogically placed
in case of emergency.

LAST WORD

In a room full of your acquaintances
examining me,
analyzing me,
whispering about me,
I was Black enough
to carry your love around gracefully;
to fend off so called friends who came onto me,
to worry about those knocks on your door,
and to wonder who you were hiding from.

I was Black enough
to drive back and forth to your place
six times in two hours
so you wouldn't be concerned about me
the night my phone was disconnected.

To ask you to be honest with me
about what you really wanted
to accomplish with your life
once all the 'shit' had passed
so that you could feel safe enough
to go out in the open again.

To understand even now,
that being Black enough
had nothing to do with the problems
between you and me,
even though you used it to defend your leaving.

Baby, I was Black enough
and fool enough
to still love the hell out of you
on those clandestine nights,
when you were talking Black to me,
but not acting particularly beautiful.

NYC

Man oh man,
it was cold there
and damp.
I felt like rotted garbage
in a wet bag.
It was chilling
when people would brush past me.
Annoyed shoulders
passing by
in crowd
after crowd
after crowd.

I was crying
and no one there
said love to me,
hardly ever.

That's why
I left.

ROBB, THE LAST TIME

Early fall
I was doing 58
in a 30,
trying to
beat the light.
Fate,
though barely a notion,
assured that the red got me.
Knowing the wait to be
longer than usual, I must have
huffed in characteristic impatience.
Undoubtedly, I sat back disgusted,
and likely I crossed my arms over my chest
just as I always do.

To my left
a big, black, macho pickup approached
and eased to a gentle stop beside me.
When the horn blew,
my disgust was dipped in venom.
I could hardly bother
to glance over.
But I did and noticed him
Smiling at me broadly.
He leaned over and rolled
his window down.

Salt and pepper hair fell
across his tanned forehead.
His blue eyes twinkled mischievously.
He was wearing a red tee shirt
and a worn black leather jacket
A man's man,
fine as always
looking good
with no effort at all.
His beauty should have been illegal
in every state.
He was well-travelled
and blessed with natural charm.

Exuberantly he hailed me,
shouting over a deep throated motor,
*"Hey girl, you're looking good. It's been
too long since we partied."*

"Hey fine thing," I said smiling back,
"and which fool let you out on this beautiful day?"

"Working for a living." he told me as the light turned green.
He put his hand to his ear,
making the universal sign for CALL ME
and waved good-bye.

With the sun shining
we pulled away and drove our separate ways.
I remember thinking
how much I always enjoyed being around him.
A genuinely nice man, so fun, so real.
I made a promise to myself to
see him more often.

Six months later,
a hard winter was losing its grip.
I got a call from our mutual friend.
She had been keeping me appraised
of the changes to the world which
we once thought we knew so well.
"Robb passed away last night" she said,
"he went peacefully."

It was his decision not to wage war
against that which was inevitable.
"You wouldn't have recognized him"' she told me.
It was neither claim, nor comfort,
just a simple truth.
This plague
leaves beauty ravaged in it's wake.
It has no mercy
and makes no exception.

I realize now
how lucky I was
to have been given
this memory of him
smiling at me
that September afternoon.
As I drive by
I selfishly replay those few small moments
and cherish them
each and every time
I cross that little intersection.

NOTES TO A MAN FRIEND

Finding out
that you had killed yourself last year
took me by sorrowful surprise.
But when I heard them say,
"It was probably one of his fantasies!"
well, they carried it too far.
It reached into my gut
and squeezed a piece of anger out of me.
This made me realize
how lonely it must have been for you.
You spent your life
surrounded by so called men
who have debased real emotion
into such infantile degradation
that even your death does not
limit their opportunity to
inflict further humiliation.
I know
this was love you were doing
my sensitive friend
and
that last act of desperation
was only an attempt
to express the need
to show us
what you felt inside
was real and could not be ignored.
Even if it was not
their idea of
a manly thing to do.

SENSITIVE WOMAN

I am a sensitive woman.
Not always secure in what I feel.
I am a sensitive woman
but do not try to use that to hold me back.

I can also be forceful
and stubborn,
with a tendency to come on too strong.

Yes, I have my weaker moments
when you can sucker me into thinking
that you really care.

But I am also a proud woman
destined to become more.
I am growing,
learning,
accommodating,
and willing to share.

I am first a woman,
and then
sensitive.

So, let me advise you now,
just because I am a woman
living in a time of change
I may be prone to bending over backward
to believe in you.
Don't let me find out otherwise.
Because
sensitivity aside,
I may also be apt
to bite you back.

COMPLICATIONS

When you reach higher
than your love can hold on to,
something inside
mashes down
in the bottom of your stomach.

When you want more
than your love can provide you
everything inside
rumbles.
All your resolutions quake.

When you give more,
than you get from,
harsh realization
drips into the hollow places
in your heart.

I am talking about
being on that two way street,
alone.

When it's not right
you know it.
Though you may fight it
and try to hold on,
when it's not right
inside you know
and
it cannot be denied.

LEGAL TENDER

There is consolation squeezed
from my bitter presumption
that the radios still play our song
on the street where you live.
Occasionally,
I do extract uneasy retribution
from my hopeful assumption,
that whenever you hear that song
it still rocks you hard
in the places you have neglected to cover.
I do also admit to having entertained
vengeful delusions
of you standing with a cup of morning coffee,
being taken by surprise
that the sound can still bring you down.
No, I don't feel embarrassed
that I make such conclusions.
This despondent repast
has helped me get through it.
I am comforted to believe,
despite your stupid pretensions,
somewhere out there
our tune plays on.
If there's a God
I wish you overwhelming vexation
because I want to believe
for moments in time
you hunger still
for my special sensation.
You can call it protection.
You can call it surrender.
I choose to see it
as due legal tender.

TURN UP THE MUSIC

I did not intend to become responsible
for anything or anybody,
let alone myself.
The plan (loosely speaking)
was centered around my own
hassle-free existence.
I was born to live
for the next party,
and if the party didn't come, well,
I could be a party all my own.

Then,
I fell in love and
got religion.
Now it's nine to five
no time for drinking.

The taxes are due in fourteen days.
I just did make the car payment
and the man is coming round tomorrow
to collect his rent.
I got a stack of bills marked TO PAY,
my mama wants to know
when I'm going to fly down her way,
My sweetheart told me I'm not much fun
cause my loving, just isn't what it usta be.

Down the hall
I can hear Aretha singing
but I can't identify that song.
I got my head in my hands Chile'
wishing hard that somebody
would turn up the music.

FIESTA

It was nice sharing hot sun,
billowy clouds,
and banana-berry smoothies with you
while walking through a populated maze
of artistic interpretations.
We offered up our own interconnected
explanations to each other,
dabbling in past and present like
multicolored swatches swirling around
our yet to come.
It was nice in the long run
deciding that I was right again,
I don't have to categorize myself for you,
though I guess I wound up trying to anyway
cause somehow (though I can't figure it out)
the need to have you understand is real.
So in words and pictures
long walks and shoreline talks
I offered up to you my own montage.
Who I am
is me and naturally I have many colors
some loud, some muted, some shades of gray.
Who I am is I,
mixed media, assemblage, words on a page.
My experiences united to form significance.
I am me
already formed,
still in the making,
firm yet pliable
I think you understand now,
I hope you do
cause what I think I heard you say
is
your hues
are many too.

RUSH

You come to my thoughts
everyday
just before the hour,
just after the hour,
right between the minutes.
I can sense the rush of wanting you.

You come to my house
full speed
sprinkling rose petals
across my front steps,
talking confidently of making changes
to my sullen demeanor
and the way I smoke too many Merits
to take any low tar compensation.

You come to my door
hesitant and vulnerable
with streetwise questions
in your eyes which tell me
you too are running scared from somewhere else.
You are unsure of my overt intentions.

I push my luck
pressing hard against your soft mouth
and surrender is all around us.

We come to each other
no intensity forced.
Between us lies the power
for intentional changes.
I am not who I was Love,
and neither,
I hope,
are you.

PRELUDES

I am that
gentle woman lady
who could lie between your thighs
like a petal suspended on a stem.

I could drink up
your warm love
in great big gulps and
quench a strong, insatiable thirst.

I could cover your skin
with all the softness
of my brown body and
swallow the love you give me whole.

Like a drowning soul
clinging to a life raft
so too would I cling to you.

Honey inside me
it feels like
a million strings
are pulling at my heart.

Here, suddenly,
I have stopped to see you
in the light.

I finally understand now,
that the things
I am feeling for you
are beautiful
tender
woman feelings
of love.

SPAROW CONTEMPLATES THE SEASONS

The sunshine of tomorrow
is not promised to us,
but the radiance of your winning smile
warms my days and all my evenings.
Everything you touched in me
has bloomed.

Your love awakened
my sedentary life,
and ended the slumber and sadness
of my past discontent.
The days you make now,
carry me into a lush and beautiful garden.

I grow here,
nurtured,
and happy.

Although I might only have you
in my life
for now,
know that in no way,
will this make me turn
and walk away.

Instead
I will hold your strong hand tightly.
You hold mine
just the same.

We'll go forward,
And speak casually
making next summer's plans.

We'll share a walk on the hillside
And note that it is
Turning brilliant colors
All around us.

Our pleasures,
Simple.

Our optimism,
Brazen.

Our expectations,
Ever hopeful.

On such gifted afternoons
I will hide my little fears
and do as you desire.

Though winter may
lay before us
let winter come, love
as
winters come.

I will love you,
deeply
fully
bravely
all the more through winter,
come what may.

MIDNIGHT HOUR

In the midnight hour
we are holding one another closely.
Darkness covers us
from the world outside.
No strangers touch
on this good night.
I lay my head on your shoulder
and listen silently
as you begin to tell me
your life story.
These intimate disclosures
clarify my prior definitions.
I am led to understanding
who you really are, and why.
Whatever I had thought
or did not think
must now include these tender scars.
I pull you closer
and offer reassurance to your
journey back in time.
This mending mission elevates me
from sexual partner to lover,
one who comprehends the hidden meanings
and the sensitive connections.
In the midnight hour
I realize the treasure of
these quiet whispers and
on this night
my love grows to include
the person you have finally let me see.
No strangers touch
on an evening of verbal surrender.
Who we are and what we might become
has everything to do with the sharing of
such precious moments.

THE ART OF LEAVING IN THE MORNING

Stretching
I discover you by my side.
I take brief seconds
for recollection.

You stare at me,
my arms fold across my breast defensively.
I murmur my most casual
GOOD MORNING,
knowing full well
I always look like hell
in the AM.

I have an overwhelming desire
to flee this strange apartment.
I wish that you were still asleep
so I could slip away quietly and go home.
NO THANKS, I CAN'T SMOKE THIS EARLY,
MY CHEST HURTS. NO COFFEE THANKS, NO
NOTHINGS THE MATTER. I GUESS I'D BETTER BE
GOING...

What do you mean I make you feel cheap.
Isn't this what I'm supposed to do now?
We both
enjoyed last night
but part of the deal is
knowing when to go home, right?

Surely, you are not the kind who
wants to hear my problems.
Surely, you are not someone who
may actually turn out to care.

You see,
I hate
one night stands.
This game called intimate strangers.

What I really, really want is
someone who won't have to say
"I'll call you tomorrow..."

What I really, really need is
somewhere I can stay
with somebody I can make love with
all day long,
the morning be damned.

SHE IS HERE

She is here
despite what you say.
She is here
and I see her.
Why can't you?
She is
lurking ever ready in that special pen.
She is
harmonizing with you on that certain CD
(last song, disc two).
She is
in the way that you pour my wine
doing your classy waiter routine.
She is
in your sock drawer
in that inventive way you fold your argyles.
She caused you to put cream in my coffee.
When you know, I like it black.
She is in our nighttime when I feel you dream her.
She was first, I am another and
I know this.
She will always be here
in the ways that she affected you.
So do not try to tell me that
she is
a thing of the past.
We both know
she is one
who loved you so much
it left behind strong impressions.

I will not deny that woman
her due recognition.
I can see, in her own way,
she must have loved you very hard.

CONFLICT

Can't talk to you,
can't try.
Though I want to I can't cause
I don't want to
want to,
but I do
so I can't and
I hope you'll understand.
I must try to live
without you
because I know that I would have to
because I know that I can't have you
because I know that I will always want to
because I know that I never will.

So I won't call you
and I can't see you,
because I do love you
and I can't just love you
because I know that
merely loving you
could never be enough
to keep me satisfied.

Life's a bitch when
you have to compromise.
When you don't want to
but you do.
When you would have to
so you won't.
Because half enough
ain't good enough,
and twice as hard as
dealing with
none at all.

LOVING YOUR BEHIND

It's bad enough
that I have to go through
getting over you
by myself.
Don't make it worse
by treating me so incidentally.
Leave me some dignity.
Enough to maintain the illusion
that you really did understand
about love
and
my stupid feelings.
Go on and go then,
if going is what your impulses demand.
Just don't act such the fool
it makes me start to
question my own judgment.
I know I'm being left
and I'll be nice enough
not to ask you for the gritty details.
I just want you to behave as though
it really matters to you,
that you leave me
still proud that I
ever loved your behind
in the first place.

AN UNFORESEEN CIRCUMSTANCE

Any other time,
I would have been
taking flying lessons,
or taking a class,
or taking something.
Any other time,
I would never have
been caught with
my emotions exposed.
I would have had a diversion.
With plenty on my mind
to occupy me.
But your
dazzling departure,
with no hint of goodbye,
caught me still in my bathrobe
speechless and peeking
through the Venetian blinds.

THE LAST OF YOU

Sirens scream around my corner.
Spectators gather to watch.
The excitement brews.
Small children dodge playfully
among the restless crowd.
The loud murmur of voices rises.
And suddenly cheers break from the throng
that surrounds me.

As I pick up my pen,
silence descends,
save a few OOOHS and AAAHS
when I reach for a piece of paper.

Anticipation peaks
to a fervored pitch
and I gather all my composure.

Then,
with nerves of steel,
I proceed
through deafening applause
to write
the last
of you.

GROWN UP CONCLUSIONS

These times
remind me
of being sixteen
and writing covert poems
to expose fragile young feelings.

Of being stuck
in the bowels of the city subway
when the lights went out.

There is some real gut wrenching fear here
in these grown up conclusions.

Each word is
a new discovery.
All thoughts are
potentially explosive.

I am wrapped up in
this emotional bind
and conflicting feelings
record themselves.

Tonight in my silence
I lay tucked in tightly
afraid of tomorrow,
unsure.

There is no sleep
on Goodman Street.

I ponder.

TROUBLES

I have
trials
and tribulations.
I have
emotional jams
that tie up
all my free ways.
I have
bad days
and
moody ways
and some days when
I don't even like me.
So,
what do you want to be
loving me for, Sugar?
Can't you see
I've got
enough troubles.

LIFE'S WORK

I am
like a
crazed sculptor.
Chipping
and
chiseling
toward a
perfect form.
There are
times though,
when I
long to
lay down
this pen,
and
have
somebody
admire
all that
has been
uncovered
thus far.

PEN IS STUCK

My pen is stuck
it will not write
flowery passages for me.
It will not transcribe
these strange feelings into nicely packaged poetics
and ease my mind of it's heavy burdens.
There are no lines that
I can write to feel better.
Something is wrong here
in this Oz within me.
Familiar things
have diminished strength to hold me.
Still, I do not know what it is
that I am rebelling against.
How does one create perfection?
What is it that I need
or don't need
that strangles me?

My dark spaces surround me
while jumbled words gag me.
Inside I feel like a dictionary
with all the pages
scattered about.

TESTIFY

Write pretty poems
so I can show them to my friends.
Girl,
you spend too much time
dealing in this soul search.
I think if you would concentrate
on things that are more poetic, well
you could probably make something
out of yourself.
People get tired
of reading about
somebody doing you wrong.
I'm telling you
what you need to do is
write some pretty poems
cause that's where
the money is.

SIMPLE

Simple?
Ha-Ha

Yeah man,
this is
SO-O-O
simple.

It just r-r-rolls right on my paper.

At one AM
when I am tired,
and lonesome,
and hurting,
and the blues have me
craving morning light.

Yeah,
okay, it's true.
Anyone else could
feel this way.

SO-O-O
No there isn't any secret
to poetic inspiration.
Yeah, you are right,
any old body
could write this stuff.

Feeling it is
SO-O-O
simple.
Yeah man,
and what I've been trying to tell you is,
this somebody did.

www.ingramcontent.com/pod-product-compliance
Lightning Source LLC
Chambersburg PA
CBHW020017050426
42450CB00005B/523